Texas A&M
Aggies
TRIVIA CHALLENGE

SOURCEBOOKS, INC.
NAPERVILLE, ILLINOIS

Copyright © 2008 by Sourcebooks, Inc.
Cover and internal design © 2008 by Sourcebooks, Inc.
Cover images © AP Images

All rights reserved. No part of this book may be reproduced in any form or by any electronic or mechanical means including information storage and retrieval systems—except in the case of brief quotations embodied in critical articles or reviews—without permission in writing from its publisher, Sourcebooks, Inc.

All brand names and product names used in this book are trademarks, registered trademarks, or trade names of their respective holders. Sourcebooks, Inc., is not associated with any product or vendor in this book.

Published by Sourcebooks, Inc.
P.O. Box 4410, Naperville, Illinois 60567-4410
(630) 961-3900
Fax: (630) 961-2168
www.sourcebooks.com

Printed and bound in Canada
WC 10 9 8 7 6 5 4 3 2 1

Texas A&M has a long football history remarkable not just for its statistical records and milestone victories, but also for the wealth of player and fan traditions recognized as some of the greatest in college football. Aggie lore is rich with rites of passage like the Boot Line and long-running rivalries, as with Texas. Kyle Field has been a stopping point for some of the greatest coaches in college history—as well as a launching pad for some of the most successful careers in the NFL. Now, in 2008, the Aggies are set to begin a new era with a new coach—but familiar face—and one that promises to bring new traditions to an already-storied past.

These 200 questions should test your knowledge of all of it, from all-time passing records to once-in-a-lifetime game-winning plays. From the quirky comments famous coaches have made to the game-day traditions cooked up by the crowd. If you're both a stat geek and a passionate fan, you should be able to get to the last page without clicking on your browser or calling a classmate. The questions and topics are designed to grow tougher, taking you from the big records and names to the obscure and bizarre. Get half of the answers right, and the Junction Boys would probably still be proud!

MIKE SHERMAN

1. **In November of 2007, Mike Sherman was hired as the _____ head coach in Texas A&M history.**
   a. 12th
   b. 17th
   c. 22nd
   d. 28th

2. **What job had Sherman been doing just before he was hired as A&M's football coach?**
   a. head coach of the Houston Texans
   b. offensive coordinator of the Houston Texans
   c. head coach of the Green Bay Packers
   d. offensive coordinator of the Seattle Seahawks

3. **Sherman had previously been tied to the Aggie program as _____.**
   a. a player in the 1970s
   b. the recruiting coordinator in the late 1980s
   c. an assistant coach in the 1990s
   d. an NFL scout responsible for in-state schools for the Texans

4. **Where did Sherman have his own college playing career?**
   a. Texas A&M
   b. Central Connecticut State
   c. Tulane
   d. Holy Cross

5. **Earlier in his career, Sherman worked with which one-time Texas A&M head coach while at another institution?**
   a. Bear Bryant
   b. Jackie Sherrill
   c. Gene Stallings
   d. Emory Bellard

TRADITIONS

6. Texas A&M is located in which Texas town?
 a. College Station
 b. Austin
 c. Lubbock
 d. Waco

7. What is the name of the annual Texas A&M spring game?
 a. the Offense–Defense Game
 b. the Spring Intrasquad Game
 c. the Maroon and White Game
 d. the Spring Shirts Game

8. The Aggie football fan base is often called _____.
 a. the 12th man
 b. the invisible player
 c. the maroon wave
 d. the Monday morning quarterback

9. What is the name of the Texas A&M band?
 a. The Big Band from Aggieland
 b. The Baddest Band in Texas
 c. The Fightin' Texas Aggie Band
 d. The Million Marching Aggies

10. What is the name of Texas A&M's official fight song?

a. "Aggie War Hymn"
b. "Spirit of Aggieland"
c. "Goodbye to Texas University"
d. "Aggie Recall"

11. According to the lyrics, the Texas Aggies are "the boys who _____."

a. know the way to win
b. show the real old fight
c. know how to down the Longhorns
d. will win on any day

12. The Texas A&M marching band is _____.

a. the largest military marching band in the country
b. the oldest marching band in college football
c. the largest marching band in college football
d. older than the football team at Texas A&M

13. What is the name of the pep rally held before each A&M game?

a. Gig 'Em Practice
b. Aggie War Cry
c. Midnight Yell Practice
d. Aggie Cheer Drill

14. What does the "gig 'em" sign look like?

a. a thumbs-up
b. a pumped fist
c. a boot kick
d. a peace sign

15. Who gets to line up in the Boot Line?

a. walk-ons
b. special-teams players
c. senior cadets
d. former football players

16. What is Reveille?

   a. a golden retriever
   b. a collie
   c. a cocker spaniel
   d. a beagle

17. During the 2008 season, Texas A&M will be debuting the latest mascot, _____.

   a. Reveille V
   b. Reveille VI
   c. Reveille VII
   d. Reveille VIII

18. When the first Reveille died in 1944, she was _____.

   a. taxidermized and placed in the team locker room
   b. given a formal military funeral
   c. posthumously promoted to a five-star general
   d. given an all-night candlelight vigil

19. Where did the name Reveille come from?

   a. It was already the name of A&M's first mascot when she was adopted at the pound.
   b. It was the Corps Commandant's favorite song, and he named the dog.
   c. The original Reveille had a way of waking the cadets up in the morning—the same way the song is intended to.
   d. After she was first brought to campus by some cadets, she started barking during the playing of Reveille.

20. How did maroon become one of the school colors?

   a. A&M's first football coach wanted to emulate the college football power at the time—the University of Chicago.
   b. It was the favorite color of the first university president's wife, because of the maroon wildflowers that grew in the area.
   c. It was elected by a vote of the student body in 1911 over gold, royal blue, and scarlet.
   d. In the 1920s, a uniform supplier accidentally sent maroon jerseys when the team had actually been wearing red and white.

21. From 1972 to 1978, instead of maroon, the Aggies' helmets were what color?

   a. black
   b. gold
   c. white
   d. silver

22. Bear Bryant once said "10 Aggies can yell louder than _____."

   a. a whole herd of longhorns
   b. a hundred of anybody else
   c. 10 fighter jets taking off
   d. 100 coaches when the game is on the line

A FORMER TRADITION

23. For years Texas A&M students commemorated the football season with a _____.

    a. torchlight parade
    b. bonfire
    c. cookout
    d. rally

24. Which year did that tradition begin?

    a. 1894
    b. 1909
    c. 1928
    d. 1941

25. What was the tradition originally intended to symbolize?

    a. the Aggies' "burning desire" to beat Texas
    b. the "eternal light" of Aggie tradition
    c. the "white-hot pride" of Aggie students and alumni
    d. the "intense feeling" between A&M and all of its rivals

26. An old Aggie myth states that Texas A&M would win the game against Texas if _____.

    a. the students camped around the bonfire through the entire night
    b. the bonfire took less than one minute to ignite
    c. the players joined their fans at the bonfire lighting
    d. the bonfire burned until after midnight

27. **Why was the bonfire built but torn down in 1963—the first year since its inception that it was NOT lit?**
    a. The students did not light it as a protest against the pending Vietnam war.
    b. A recent spate of bush fires in Texas caused the university to cancel the fire.
    c. It was a tribute to John F. Kennedy, who had been assassinated.
    d. It was in honor of the first astronauts who died in training for the Project Apollo.

28. **The bonfire tradition was halted after a tragedy in the preparation for the event killed 12 students and alumni in which year?**
    a. 1997
    b. 1999
    c. 2000
    d. 2002

29. **Those Aggies are remembered _____.**
    a. with a retired jersey number for each student
    b. with a memorial dedicated in 2004
    c. with a prayer said before each Texas game
    d. with a row of empty seats in the student section

KYLE FIELD

30. What is the capacity of Kyle Field?

 a. 65,050
 b. 74,900
 c. 82,600
 d. 91,400

31. Who was E.J. Kyle?

 a. Texas A&M's first university president
 b. the Texas A&M booster who funded the stadium's original construction
 c. Texas A&M's third football coach
 d. Texas A&M's first dean of the school of agriculture

32. The Aggies have been playing on the Kyle Field site since _____.

 a. 1899
 b. 1905
 c. 1916
 d. 1927

33. The first real stadium at the site was completed in which year?

 a. 1910
 b. 1929
 c. 1935
 d. 1948

34. How much did its construction cost at the time?

a. $3,000
b. $36,000
c. $136,000
d. $365,000

35. Starting during the 1990 season, the Aggies won how many consecutive games at Kyle Field?

a. 16
b. 22
c. 31
d. 40

36. As of 2007, Kyle Field is the largest football stadium _____.

a. in Texas
b. in the South
c. west of the Mississippi
d. in Div. I college football

37. What happened to Kyle Field in 1996?

a. An electronic scoreboard was installed for the first time.
b. The light standards were turned on for the first time.
c. The artificial turf was restored to natural grass.
d. The stadium had its first sell-out at expanded capacity.

38. Texas A&M set an attendance record at Kyle Field in 2001, when 87,555 fans turned out to see the Aggies play which opponent?

a. Texas
b. Texas Tech
c. Oklahoma
d. Nebraska

CONFERENCE PLAY

39. Which division of the Big 12 Conference does Texas A&M play in?
a. the North
b. the South
c. the East
d. the West

40. What was the first conference Texas A&M ever joined?
a. the Southern Intercollegiate Athletic Association
b. the Texas Intercollegiate Athletic Association
c. the Big South
d. the Southern Alliance of Independent Schools

41. What conference was Texas A&M a part of before it joined the Big 12?
a. the Southeastern Conference
b. the Southwest States Coalition
c. the Southern Athletic Association
d. the Southwest Conference

42. What eventually happened to that conference?
a. As a smaller conference, it was renamed the Western Athletic Conference.
b. The remaining members all became independents.
c. The remaining schools became the West Division of Conference USA.
d. It disbanded.

43. Which current Big 12 member was NOT also a part of that conference before the birth of the Big 12?

   a. Texas
   b. Texas Tech
   c. Oklahoma
   d. Baylor

44. Which year did play begin in the new Big 12 conference?

   a. 1988
   b. 1992
   c. 1996
   d. 2000

45. Where are the Big 12 headquarters located?

   a. Omaha, Nebraska
   b. Irving, Texas
   c. Norman, Oklahoma
   d. Lawrence, Kansas

46. The Big 12 conference includes schools in how many different states?

   a. 3
   b. 5
   c. 7
   d. 9

47. How many championships did Texas A&M win in the Southwest Conference?

   a. 6
   b. 12
   c. 17
   d. 23

48. Texas A&M had a long-running series with a former Southwest Conference foe that now hasn't been played since 1991, when the opponent left to play instead in the SEC. Who was the opponent?

a. LSU
b. Arkansas
c. Tennessee
d. Alabama

49. In March of 2008 the two schools announced that the series would finally resume at which neutral site?

a. the Cotton Bowl
b. the Alamodome
c. Dallas Cowboys Stadium
d. Houston's Reliant Stadium

IN-STATE RIVALS

50. What is the name of Texas A&M's annual rivalry game with Texas?

a. the Texas Take-down
b. the Lone Star Showdown
c. the Battle for the Belt Buckle
d. the Old Cowboy Rivalry

51. What year was that game first played?

a. 1883
b. 1894
c. 1901
d. 1905

52. When is that game now typically played?

a. the first Saturday of the season
b. the last Saturday of the season
c. Labor Day
d. the day after Thanksgiving

53. Rival Texas's first mascot, the original Bevo longhorn, was branded on the hide with what slogan by A&M fans in 1916?

a. the word "Aggie"
b. the score "13–0" from an A&M victory over Texas
c. the word "shutout" referring to that same victory
d. the letters A and M

54. **Texas A&M beat Texas for the second consecutive year in 2007. When was the last time the Aggies had consecutive victories over Texas?**

    a. 1999–2000
    b. 1997–1998
    c. 1991–1994
    d. 1983–1986

55. **How many touchdowns did quarterback Stephen McGee have in the 2007 victory over Texas?**

    a. 3
    b. 4
    c. 5
    d. 6

56. **What happened immediately after that game?**

    a. Dennis Franchione announced his resignation.
    b. The Cotton Bowl committee invited the Aggies to play.
    c. A brawl between Aggie and Longhorn fans broke out in the parking lot.
    d. Martellus Bennett announced that he was leaving school early for the NFL draft.

57. **Texas A&M's 16–3 win over Texas in 1986 led to the firing of which Texas head coach?**

    a. Fred Akers
    b. David McWilliams
    c. John Mackovic
    d. Darrell Royal

58. **Between 1956 and 1975, how many times did Texas A&M beat the rival Longhorns?**

    a. 0
    b. 1
    c. 10
    d. 15

59. What is the name of Texas A&M's annual game with Baylor?

a. the Battle of the Brazos
b. the Lone Star Showdown
c. the Battle for the Bones
d. the Battle of Texas-6

60. Why was that rivalry temporarily suspended after the 1926 game?

a. Baylor accused Texas A&M of stealing signs.
b. Texas A&M accused Baylor of using an ineligible player.
c. The two schools' coaches got into a fist fight after the game.
d. A violent brawl broke out among the students.

61. Why was the rivalry halted again in 1943 and 1944?

a. The two schools decided in the spirit of the unified war home front not to play what had become an increasingly nasty rivalry.
b. Both schools suspended their football programs during the war.
c. Baylor did not have a team because of the war.
d. Texas A&M wound up playing a schedule exclusively made up of military teams that year.

62. The Aggies came back from trailing 17–0 to upset Baylor, 31–30, in 1986. Quarterback Kevin Murray threw the winning touchdown with 3:48 to play to which receiver?

a. Sylvester Morgan
b. Shea Walker
c. Rod Harris
d. Tony Thompson

63. How many touchdowns was Murray responsible for in that game?

a. 3
b. 4
c. 5
d. 6

CHAMPIONSHIPS

64. As of 2008, which year did Texas A&M win its lone Associated Press national title?
   a. 1939
   b. 1954
   c. 1969
   d. 1978

65. Who coached the Aggies during the national championship season?
   a. Homer Norton
   b. Madison Bell
   c. Dana X. Bible
   d. Charley Moran

66. What was Texas A&M's record that year?
   a. 11–0
   b. 10–1
   c. 9–1–1
   d. 10–0–1

67. What was the Aggies' record the previous season?
   a. 10–1
   b. 8–2
   c. 6–4
   d. 4–4–1

68. Who did the Aggies beat in the Sugar Bowl at the end of the national championship run?

a. Alabama
b. LSU
c. Tennessee
d. Tulane

69. Who scored the winning touchdown in that game, a 14–13 come-from-behind victory that helped Texas A&M define its national reputation?

a. Marion Pugh
b. John Kimbrough
c. Tommie Vaughn
d. Joe Boyd

70. What season did the Aggies win their first Big 12 title?

a. 1997
b. 1998
c. 2001
d. 2002

71. Which team did Texas A&M beat in the conference championship game that year, in two overtimes, to win the title?

a. Oklahoma
b. Nebraska
c. Oklahoma State
d. Kansas State

72. That team held what national ranking going into the game?

a. 1st
b. 2nd
c. 5th
d. 7th

73. **The Aggies nearly lost that game on a Hail Mary at the end of regulation, but Kansas State's Everett Burnett was tackled at the 1-yard line by which A&M defender to force overtime?**

   a. Dat Nguyen
   b. Jason Webster
   c. Brandon Jennings
   d. Toya Jones

74. **In overtime, the Aggies had to trade field goals with which K-State kicker?**

   a. Martin Gramatica
   b. Adam Vinatieri
   c. Steve Christie
   d. Al Del Greco

75. **Who was on the receiving end of the winning touchdown in that game?**

   a. Leroy Hodge
   b. Chris Cole
   c. Sirr Parker
   d. Chris Taylor

76. **The Aggies won that game despite _____.**

   a. playing on K-State's home turf
   b. playing without their starting quarterback
   c. amassing 12 penalties
   d. gaining only 180 yards of total offense

77. **During Jackie Sherrill's Texas A&M tenure, the Aggies won three straight Southwest Conference championships during what years?**

   a. 1982–84
   b. 1984–86
   c. 1985–87
   d. 1987–89

HONORS

78. As of 2008, who is Texas A&M's lone Heisman Trophy winner?

a. John Kimbrough
b. Marshall Robnett
c. John David Crow
d. Darren Lewis

79. Which year did he win it?

a. 1954
b. 1956
c. 1957
d. 1959

80. He won the award that year despite _____.

a. appearing in only seven games
b. playing for a losing team
c. rushing for only 408 yards
d. being only a sophomore at the time

81. He is also the only _____ to ever win the Heisman.

a. dual running back/quarterback
b. player from a Texas school
c. native of the South
d. player under Bear Bryant

82. After winning the Heisman, that player was a first-round draft pick of which team in the 1958 NFL draft?

a. the Chicago Cardinals
b. the Green Bay Packers
c. the Philadelphia Eagles
d. the New York Giants

83. In 1940, John Kimbrough was the Heisman Trophy runner-up to which winner?

a. Michigan's Tom Harmon
b. TCU's Davey O'Brien
c. Georgia's Frank Sinkwich
d. Army's Doc Blanchard

84. Which Aggie won the Lombardi Award as the top lineman or linebacker in college football and the Bednarik Award for defensive player of the year in 1998?

a. Brandon Mitchell
b. Dat Nguyen
c. Ron Edwards
d. Brandon Jennings

85. As of 2008, how many players does Texas A&M have in the College Football Hall of Fame?

a. 4
b. 6
c. 8
d. 10

86. Who was Texas A&M's first All-American?

a. John Kimbrough
b. Joe Boyd
c. Joe Routt
d. Marshall Robnett

87. What happened to him later?

a. He was the first A&M player to return as head coach.
b. He went on to win three Super Bowl rings in the NFL.
c. He was killed in the Battle of the Bulge in World War II.
d. He became a prominent businessman in College Station with a chain of restaurants that still exists today.

88. As of 2008, who has been A&M's lone three-time All-American?

a. tailback Leeland McElroy
b. tailback Darren Lewis
c. linebacker Johnny Holland
d. cornerback Pat Thomas

89. Which of the following Texas A&M coaches is NOT in the College Football Hall of Fame, as of 2008?

a. Dana X. Bible
b. Bear Bryant
c. Jackie Sherrill
d. Homer Norton

90. Safety Dave Elmendorf was an All-American in both football and what other sport?

a. basketball
b. baseball
c. track
d. wrestling

91. Who has been A&M's only pair of brothers to both be All-Americans?

a. Darren and Courtney Lewis
b. Bill and Mike Hobbs
c. Rolf and Charlie Krueger
d. Dennis and Adam Goehring

92. Bear Bryant famously said of John David Crowe in 1957 that if the Heisman Trophy voters didn't give the Aggie tailback the honor, "_____."

a. they should stop handing out the award
b. they will have to answer to every Aggie alumni in the military today
c. I will personally show up in New York thrashing my houndstooth hat
d. we will bring all of our shiny boots to New York

HISTORY

93. Texas A&M was originally a(n) _____.

   a. naval college
   b. women's teacher's college
   c. all-male college
   d. Methodist college

94. Which year did Texas A&M University open?

   a. 1876
   b. 1884
   c. 1894
   d. 1901

95. Which year was the first football game played?

   a. 1888
   b. 1894
   c. 1899
   d. 1902

96. Who was Texas A&M's first opponent?

   a. Brazos High School
   b. Texas
   c. Baylor
   d. Austin College

97. Who was Texas A&M's first football coach?

   a. J.E. Platt
   b. C.W. Taylor
   c. F.D. Perkins
   d. C.B. Moran

98. What was Texas A&M's record in the program's first season?

   a. 0–4
   b. 1–1
   c. 3–1
   d. 5–0

99. Which year did Texas A&M have its first perfect season (8–0–0)?

   a. 1989
   b. 1904
   c. 1917
   d. 1939

100. Which year did the Aggies win their first conference championship?

   a. 1911
   b. 1917
   c. 1925
   d. 1939

101. Dana X. Bible's 1919 Texas A&M team _____.

   a. won the first national championship of the Associated Press poll
   b. was unscored on for the entire season
   c. won the first-ever Cotton Bowl
   d. set an NCAA record for most points scored in a season

102. The Aggies' November 27, 1952, game against Texas in Austin marked A&M's first _____.

   a. win against Texas on the road in 32 years
   b. night game played in any venue
   c. Southwest Conference championship
   d. televised game

103. The same two teams also met in a 1921 game that was a milestone for what reason?

a. It was the Aggies' first game broadcast on the radio.
b. It was the first game played in the new Southwest Conference.
c. It was the first game for both teams using the new forward pass.
d. It was the last game the Aggies ever played as an independent.

104. A&M's win over Fresno State on September 8, 2007, was the _____ victory in program history.

a. 500th
b. 650th
c. 700th
d. 850th

105. The 1997 game against Oklahoma State was the _____ football game played in Texas A&M history.

a. 500th
b. 1,000th
c. 1,500th
d. 2,000th

OTHER BIG GAMES

106. **Texas A&M's invitation to the Cotton Bowl at the end of the 2004 season snapped a _____ season stretch without a bowl game.**

    a. 2
    b. 3
    c. 4
    d. 5

107. **As of 2008, in which season did Texas A&M last win a bowl game?**

    a. 2004 in the Cotton Bowl
    b. 2001 in the Galleyfurniture.com Bowl
    c. 2000 in the Independence Bowl
    d. 1995 in the Alamo Bowl

108. **What was the first bowl game Texas A&M ever played in?**

    a. the Cotton Bowl
    b. the Sugar Bowl
    c. the Dixie Classic
    d. the Orange Bowl

109. **Which of the following is NOT a bowl game that the Aggies have ever played in?**

    a. the Presidential Cup Bowl
    b. the Bluebonnet Bowl
    c. the John Hancock Bowl
    d. the Tangerine Bowl

110. Which team did Texas A&M lose the 2007 Alamo Bowl to?

a. Michigan State
b. Penn State
c. Purdue
d. Northwestern

111. Texas A&M played in which bowl game six times between 1986 and 1994?

a. the Cotton Bowl
b. the Orange Bowl
c. the Alamo Bowl
d. the Sugar Bowl

112. Which No. 1 team did Texas A&M upset at home during the 2002 season?

a. Texas
b. Nebraska
c. Oklahoma
d. Oklahoma State

113. Which Aggie quarterback came off the bench in that game to score four touchdowns?

a. Dustin Long
b. Mark Farris
c. Stephen McGee
d. Reggie McNeal

114. The Aggies contained which Heisman Trophy winner in the 1986 Cotton Bowl victory?

a. Boston College's Doug Flutie
b. Auburn's Bo Jackson
c. Miami's Vinny Testaverde
d. Notre Dame's Tim Brown

115. Who coached the Aggies in the Alamo Bowl at the end of the 2007 season after Dennis Franchione had announced his resignation?

a. Franchione coached the team himself
b. new coach Mike Sherman
c. defensive coordinator Gary Darnell
d. offensive coordinator Les Koenning

INDIVIDUAL RECORDS

116. In the September 17, 2005, game against Southern Methodist, Reggie McNeal became one of the few quarterbacks in NCAA history to _____.

a. pass for five touchdowns in a single game
b. pass for 300 yards and rush for another 100
c. score a touchdown three different ways: passing, rushing, and receiving
d. pass for more than 500 yards in a single game

117. Greg Hill set an NCAA record against LSU on September 14, 1991, with the most yards gained rushing by a freshman in the first game of his college career. How many yards did he total?

a. 99
b. 159
c. 212
d. 299

118. Bill Sibley holds the NCAA record, dating back to 1941, for the most interceptions by a linebacker in a single season. How many picks did he have that year?

a. 3
b. 9
c. 16
d. 24

119. **Tony Franklin attempted 38 field goals in his career of 50 yards or longer, an NCAA record. How many of them did he make?**

    a. 8
    b. 16
    c. 24
    d. 30

120. **How many 40-plus yard field goals did Alan Smith make in the 1983 game against Arkansas State for a single-game NCAA record?**

    a. 3
    b. 4
    c. 5
    d. 6

121. **Kyle Bryant owns the longest field goal ever made in NCAA history by a freshman. How long was it?**

    a. 54 yards
    b. 57 yards
    c. 61 yards
    d. 65 yards

122. **Which Aggie All-American became the NCAA record-holder for career punt average (44.7 yards per punt)?**

    a. Steve O'Neal
    b. Tony Franklin
    c. Shane Lechler
    d. Bob Goff

123. **Who is A&M's all-time tackles leader, with 517 tackles in his career?**

    a. Brandon Mitchell
    b. Johnny Holland
    c. Dat Nguyen
    d. Sam Adams

124. Dat Nguyen set a Texas A&M record with _____ consecutive starts in his career.

a. 23
b. 35
c. 42
d. 51

125. Which Aggie had two kickoff returns for a touchdown—tied for the most in NCAA history—in a 1993 game against Rice?

a. Greg Hill
b. Leeland McElroy
c. Rodney Thomas
d. Aaron Glenn

126. As of 2008, that player also ranks third all-time in NCAA history for single season kickoff return average with how many yards per return?

a. 19
b. 29
c. 39
d. 49

127. Who holds the A&M record, as of 2008, for career tackles for loss (32)?

a. John Roper
b. Johnny Holland
c. Dat Nguyen
d. Robert Jackson

128. Who is A&M's career sacks leader (42), as of 2008?

a. Aaron Wallace
b. Johnny Holland
c. Jacob Green
d. Ray Childress

129. Which Aggie kicker became the only player in NCAA history to make two 60-yard field goals in one game, with 64- and 65-yarders against Baylor?

a. Tony Franklin
b. Terence Kitchens
c. Kyle Bryant
d. Layne Talbot

130. Who is A&M's all-time leading rusher, as of 2008, with 5,012 career yards?

a. Curtis Dickey
b. Greg Hill
c. Darren Lewis
d. Rodney Thomas

131. Who holds the record for most rushing yards in a single game, with 297 against Southern Methodist?

a. Bob Smith in 1950
b. Curtis Dickey in 1978
c. Darren Lewis in 1990
d. Leeland McElroy in 1995

132. Jorvorskie Lane tied a 79-year-old school record in 2006 with how many rushing touchdowns that season?

a. 10
b. 13
c. 19
d. 22

133. Who is A&M's career passing leader, as of 2008, with 6,992 yards?

a. Gary Kubiak
b. Corey Pullig
c. Kevin Murray
d. Reggie McNeal

134. Who holds the school record with 48 career passing touchdowns?
a. Gary Kubiak
b. Corey Pullig
c. Kevin Murray
d. Reggie McNeal

135. Who has the most career receiving yards in A&M history (2,600)?
a. Terrence Murphy
b. Bethel Johnson
c. Jamaar Taylor
d. Tony Harrison

136. Terry Venetoulias set an Aggie record converting how many consecutive extra points starting during the 1992 season?
a. 36
b. 58
c. 72
d. 101

137. Who is responsible for scoring the most points in Texas A&M history, as of the start of the 2008 season?
a. Jorvorskie Lane
b. Kyle Bryant
c. Todd Pegram
d. Rodney Thomas

138. How many interceptions did Kevin Smith have in his career for an Aggie record?
a. 10
b. 15
c. 20
d. 25

139. Joe Boring set an Aggie record with _____ interceptions in a single game against Arkansas in 1952.
a. 2
b. 3
c. 4
d. 5

MEMORABLE PLAYERS

140. Which two Aggies both rushed for at least 1,000 yards during their freshman seasons (1991 and 2003)?

   a. Darren Lewis and Bubba Bean
   b. Greg Hill and Curtis Dickey
   c. Greg Hill and Courtney Lewis
   d. Darren Lewis and Curtis Dickey

141. Which of the following players does NOT have a 100-yard kickoff return to his credit at A&M?

   a. Leeland McElroy
   b. Sirr Parker
   c. Billy Mitchell
   d. Carl Roaches

142. Which receiver had three touchdown receptions in a single game against North Texas in 1998?

   a. Chris Taylor
   b. Chris Cole
   c. Albert Connell
   d. Robert Ferguson

143. Which Aggie defender had five sacks in a single game against Houston in 1987?

   a. John Roper
   b. Alex Morris
   c. Aaron Wallace
   d. Ray Childress

144. Yale Lary was a two-sport star at Texas A&M in football and what other sport?

   a. baseball
   b. track
   c. basketball
   d. wrestling

145. What was fullback John Kimbrough's nickname?

   a. Jailor
   b. Jumpin'
   c. Joltin'
   d. Jarrin'

146. Kimbrough originally played for which school, where he was cut from the roster?

   a. Texas
   b. Tulane
   c. LSU
   d. Arkansas

147. Which future college coaching legend played one season at Texas A&M before receiving an appointment to West Point?

   a. Bobby Bowden
   b. Joe Paterno
   c. Robert Neyland
   d. Tom Osborne

148. What did "The Wrecking Crew" refer to?

   a. Texas A&M's defensive line
   b. the Aggies defense
   c. A&M's punt-blocking team
   d. A&M's scout team in practices

149. Versatile punter Shane Lechler in his career also served what role on the team?

a. backup quarterback
b. student trainer
c. wide receiver
d. kickoff coverage

150. Which two players were referred to as the "Blitz Brothers" on the 1987–88 team?

a. Johnny Holland and John Roper
b. Adam Bob and Dana Baptiste
c. Joe Johnson and Basil Jackson
d. John Roper and Aaron Wallace

151. All-American offensive tackle Maurice Moorman transferred to A&M from what program?

a. Texas
b. Kentucky
c. Oklahoma State
d. Arkansas

OTHER COACHES

152. How many seasons was Dennis Franchione the head coach at A&M?

   a. 4
   b. 5
   c. 6
   d. 7

153. What was A&M's record during his last season, in 2007?

   a 9–4
   b. 8–5
   c. 7–6
   d. 6–7

154. Which of the following is NOT a school where Franchione had also been a head coach?

   a. TCU
   b. New Mexico
   c. Pittsburg
   d. Alabama

155. Franchione was caught during the 2007 season sending _____ to select elite boosters.

   a. game tape
   b. free A&M merchandise
   c. season passes
   d. a newsletter

156. Which A&M coach has won the most games with the Aggies?

   a. Jackie Sherrill
   b. Dana X. Bible
   c. Homer Norton
   d. R.C. Slocum

157. Which two coaches share the record for longest tenure at A&M, 14 years?

a. Jackie Sherrill and Dana X. Bible
b. R.C. Slocum and Homer Norton
c. Jackie Sherrill and R.C. Slocum
d. Homer Norton and Dana X. Bible

158. Jackie Sherrill was hired in 1982 for what was then the unprecedented sum of _____.

a. $70,000
b. $98,000
c. $136,000
d. $267,000

159. What happened at the end of Sherrill's A&M tenure?

a. The Aggies won a national championship in the Coaches' Poll.
b. Sherrill developed a heart condition and decided to retire.
c. Sherrill led A&M's move into the Big 12 Conference.
d. The Aggies were placed on NCAA probation.

160. Sherrill later returned to head coaching at which school?

a. Mississippi State
b. Ole Miss
c. Arkansas
d. Alabama

161. How many seasons did Bear Bryant spend as head coach of the Aggies?

a. 3
b. 4
c. 5
d. 6

162. What was A&M's record during Bryant's first season in College Station?

a. 1–9
b. 5–5
c. 8–2
d. 9–1

163. Bryant took his team to a harsh training camp that led to the players—those who successfully completed the camp—being called _____.

a. "Bear's Boys"
b. "Bryant's Survivors"
c. "Junction Boys"
d. "Aggie Kings"

164. After Bear Bryant left, the Aggies _____ for the next nine seasons.

a. never won more than four games
b. played for the Southwest Conference title
c. offered him a contract to come back
d. had five different coaches

165. How many national championships did Bryant later win at Alabama?

a. 3
b. 4
c. 5
d. 6

166. Aside from both coaching at Texas A&M, how are Jackie Sherrill and Bear Bryant related?

a. Sherrill was an assistant coach under Bryant at Kentucky.
b. Sherrill was Bryant's own choice to replace him at Texas A&M.
c. Sherrill played for Bryant at Alabama.
d. The two developed a strong rivalry coaching against each other in the SEC.

167. How old was Gene Stallings when he became head coach at A&M in 1965?

a. 23
b. 29
c. 37
d. 42

168. Stallings returned to college football as the head coach at what other university, nearly two decades after leaving Texas A&M?

a. LSU
b. Arkansas
c. Tennessee
d. Alabama

169. Dana X. Bible coached the Aggies in 1917 and then again from 1919 until 1928. Why didn't he coach in 1918?

a. Texas A&M did not field a football program because of the war.
b. Bible briefly left for Nebraska, changed his mind, and returned.
c. Bible became A&M's athletic director for that one season.
d. Bible himself served in the war.

170. Bible also coached which two other sports at Texas A&M?

a. baseball and basketball
b. men's and women's basketball
c. baseball and track
d. basketball and wrestling

171. Bible is credited with also turning which two other schools into national football powers?

a. Oklahoma and Nebraska
b. Nebraska and Texas
c. Alabama and Oklahoma
d. TCU and Texas

172. Which of the following coaches was also a player at Texas A&M?

a. Gene Stallings
b. Homer Norton
c. Emory Bellard
d. Charley Moran

IN THE PROS

173. How many Aggies were taken in the 2008 NFL draft?

   a. 1
   b. 3
   c. 5
   d. 7

174. Who was the highest Aggie drafted?

   a. Cody Wallace
   b. Martellus Bennett
   c. Chris Harrington
   d. Red Bennett

175. Which team drafted him?

   a. the Dallas Cowboys
   b. the Tampa Bay Buccaneers
   c. the New England Patriots
   d. the Indianapolis Colts

176. Who were Texas A&M's two first-round draft picks in 2003?

   a. Ty Warren and Sammy Davis
   b. Ty Warren and Bethel Johnson
   c. Sammy Davis and Terrence Kiel
   d. Bethel Johnson and Robert Ferguson

177. **Those two players were the first Aggies drafted in the first round since _____.**

    a. 1998
    b. 1996
    c. 1994
    d. 1990

178. **Texas A&M has had three first-round draft picks once, as of 2008. Which year was that?**

    a. 1999
    b. 1994
    c. 1976
    d. 1958

179. **The most Aggies ever taken in a single year of the NFL draft were selected in 1976. How many A&M players were drafted that year, through 14 rounds?**

    a. 7
    b. 10
    c. 13
    d. 15

180. **As of 2008, who is Texas A&M's one player in the Pro Football Hall of Fame?**

    a. John David Crow
    b. John Kimbrough
    c. Dale Elmendorf
    d. Yale Lary

181. **Which NFL team drafted Dat Nguyen out of A&M in the third round of the 1999 draft?**

    a. the Miami Dolphins
    b. the Chicago Bears
    c. the Dallas Cowboys
    d. the Seattle Seahawks

182. How many seasons did All-American defensive end Jacob Green go on to play in the NFL?

a. 3
b. 6
c. 9
d. 12

183. How many career sacks did he accumulate in that time in the pros?

a. 54
b. 78
c. 116
d. 159

184. All-American safety Tommy Maxwell later won a Super Bowl with which team?

a. the Indianapolis Colts
b. the Chicago Bears
c. the Miami Dolphins
d. the Dallas Cowboys

185. All-American Steve O'Neal later set an NFL record in 1969 with a _____ punt.

a. 57-yard
b. 68-yard
c. 79-yard
d. 98-yard

186. Yale Lary later led which team to three NFL championships?

a. the Chicago Cardinals
b. the Green Bay Packers
c. the Minnesota Vikings
d. the Detroit Lions

187. How many times was Lary a Pro Bowl selection in his NFL career?

   a. 3
   b. 5
   c. 7
   d. 9

188. What was Yale Lary's given first name?

   a. Daniel
   b. Robert
   c. Stephen
   d. Joshua

189. How many interceptions did Lary have in his NFL career?

   a. 25
   b. 50
   c. 75
   d. 100

190. Lary was also known—both professionally and in college—as a great _____.

   a. player-coach
   b. punter
   c. singer
   d. wide receiver

TEAM RECORDS & DISTINCTIONS

191. During the 2004 season, Texas A&M played three overtime contests in four games against which opponents?

a. Colorado, Baylor, and Texas Tech
b. Clemson, Kansas State, and Colorado
c. Oklahoma, Texas Tech, and Texas
d. Baylor, Oklahoma, and Texas

192. Texas A&M played what rated as the toughest schedule in the country in _____.

a. 2002
b. 2004
c. 2005
d. 2006

193. What was the Aggies' record that season?

a. 9–3
b. 8–4
c. 7–5
d. 6–6

194. Texas A&M led the nation in total defense (fewest average yards allowed per game) in which year?

a. 1979
b. 1985
c. 1991
d. 1998

195. **The Aggies set an NCAA record that still stands in 2008, running up 319 yards of _____ against North Texas in 1946.**

    a. first-half total offense
    b. first-quarter total offense
    c. total rushing yardage
    d. punt-return yardage

196. **In 1968, Texas A&M and Arkansas played 184 plays in a single game without a _____ for an NCAA record.**

    a. forward pass
    b. turnover
    c. penalty
    d. punt

197. **As of the 2008 season, the Aggies have an all-time winning record against all of the following schools but one. Which one did they lose to?**

    a. Arkansas
    b. Houston
    c. Southern Methodist
    d. Texas Tech

198. **As of the 2008 season, Texas A&M has never played _____.**

    a. Purdue
    b. Michigan
    c. Wisconsin
    d. Iowa

199. As of 2008, when was the Aggies' last perfect season?

a. 1998
b. 1985
c. 1956
d. 1939

200. Which Aggie team was ranked No. 1 in the country late in the season before losing its last three games?

a. 1982
b. 1976
c. 1957
d. 1948

ANSWERS

1. d)	22. b)	43. c)	64. a)
2. b)	23. b)	44. c)	65. a)
3. c)	24. b)	45. b)	66. a)
4. b)	25. a)	46. c)	67. d)
5. b)	26. d)	47. c)	68. d)
6. a)	27. c)	48. b)	69. b)
7. c)	28. b)	49. c)	70. b)
8. a)	29. b)	50. b)	71. d)
9. c)	30. c)	51. b)	72. a)
10. a)	31. d)	52. d)	73. d)
11. b)	32. b)	53. b)	74. a)
12. a)	33. b)	54. c)	75. c)
13. c)	34. d)	55. b)	76. b)
14. a)	35. c)	56. a)	77. c)
15. c)	36. a)	57. a)	78. c)
16. b)	37. c)	58. b)	79. c)
17. d)	38. a)	59. a)	80. a)
18. b)	39. b)	60. d)	81. d)
19. d)	40. a)	61. c)	82. a)
20. d)	41. d)	62. d)	83. a)
21. c)	42. d)	63. b)	84. b)

85. c)	114. b)	143. b)	172. a)
86. c)	115. c)	144. a)	173. c)
87. c)	116. b)	145. d)	174. b)
88. b)	117. c)	146. b)	175. a)
89. c)	118. b)	147. c)	176. a)
90. b)	119. b)	148. b)	177. b)
91. c)	120. c)	149. a)	178. b)
92. a)	121. c)	150. d)	179. b)
93. c)	122. c)	151. b)	180. d)
94. a)	123. c)	152. b)	181. c)
95. b)	124. d)	153. c)	182. d)
96. d)	125. b)	154. c)	183. c)
97. c)	126. c)	155. d)	184. a)
98. b)	127. a)	156. d)	185. d)
99. c)	128. a)	157. b)	186. d)
100. b)	129. a)	158. d)	187. d)
101. b)	130. c)	159. d)	188. b)
102. d)	131. a)	160. a)	189. b)
103. a)	132. c)	161. b)	190. b)
104. b)	133. d)	162. a)	191. a)
105. b)	134. c)	163. c)	192. b)
106. a)	135. a)	164. a)	193. c)
107. b)	136. c)	165. d)	194. c)
108. c)	137. b)	166. c)	195. d)
109. d)	138. c)	167. b)	196. b)
110. b)	139. c)	168. d)	197. a)
111. a)	140. c)	169. d)	198. c)
112. c)	141. c)	170. a)	199. d)
113. d)	142. b)	171. b)	200. c)